# *Break*throughs and *Begin*nings

# *Break*throughs and *Beginnings*

A JOURNAL FOR SELF-DISCOVERY
THROUGH GROUNDING, REFLECTION,
AND AWAKENING

PHOENIX BRUHL

Books may be purchased in quantity and/or special sales by contacting the publisher.

Mynd Matters Publishing
2690 Cobb Pkwy SE, Suite A5-375
Smyrna, GA 30080
www.myndmatterspublishing.com

MYND MATTERS IS A REGISTERED TRADEMARK

ISBN: 978-1-963874-23-5 (pbk)

FIRST EDITION

*Dedicated to my family, friends, chosen family, and my future self.*

# Letter to the Reader

One day I saw a viral video of former NFL athlete Trent Shelton that was quite hard hitting.

*"Certain things fall apart for better things to fall into place. Sometimes it takes losing what you're settling for to remind you of what you truly deserve. Sometimes it takes the most uncomfortable paths to lead your life to the most beautiful place. I know it's hard, but you'll never see the purpose of the storm until you see the growth it produced. You'll never see the purpose of someone leaving your life until you see what's best for your life. You'll never understand why you're going through what you're going through until you see the strength, the power, the growth, that it built inside of you. Your current situation is not your final destination. This storm will eventually run out of rain. This struggle that seems like it lasted forever will eventually run out of pain. This hurt you, will turn into the greatest you. This broken you, will turn into the best you. Let these hard times, the hardest times in your life, turn into your best life. Let these bad days create your best days…this chapter is not your story. This moment is not your identity. This pain is not your life.*

*You have to believe the tables of your life will turn. This pain will become power. This weakness will become strength. This confusion will become peace. Better things are coming for your life. Your heart will heal. Your tears will dry. Your mind will calm. This storm will end. It will take time, but I promise you things will get better. Everything you're going through will eventually turn into everything you made it through. Never forget that every single day is a new beginning."*

We all have pivot moments in our lives. Times when we are on the cusp of something greater than our current situation would lead us to believe. I've had those moments more than I can count. I'm currently in a season of rediscovering myself again.

*Breakthroughs and Beginnings* is meant to help you reflect and recognize your thoughts and feelings by sharing some of my personal experiences and thoughts, then you can decide what to do next. Including when and how to pivot, if you need to pivot at all.

Journaling has enhanced my life. It allows me to express myself and is a healthy outlet. It is more than a routine, but a ritual that helps me get grounded. I hope this journal gives you hope, the courage to find yourself again (and again), and your voice.

Take time for yourself.

Do that bucket list thing.

Live.

*Breakthroughs and Beginnings* is a passion project. Up until now, I didn't know anything about publishing. Creating a journal was something I've always wanted to do. It's my way of contributing to a greater purpose. So, if I can just connect with and help one person—it is already worth it. I am here for you.

There are no rules for this journey. Reflect and write in any order you choose. Surrender and just let it flow.

Love and light,

*Phoenix*

# Authenticity

I am told that authenticity is the highest form of vibrational frequency. IYKYK. One of my friends is excellent at this. Well, she is actually more like a soul sister. I am amazed by how she is her authentic self... effortlessly. She is creative, driven, knows what she wants (and doesn't), loves deeply, and cares about and protects her people ferociously. She is sweet, kind, and such a joy to talk to and be around. She's the epitome of good energy. She calls it like it is. Conversely, I'm an overthinker and I'd like to get better at *being* vs thinking. The times I am being my truest self is when I notice people and situations respond in the best ways.


***Tell me about your authentic self:***

# Gratitude

Living in gratitude is more than a practice for me—it's how I live. I appreciate everything from the miniscule to the big, including my health, family and friends, opportunities, the things that didn't happen, and social invites that help me experience connection.

*What are you most grateful for? In what ways do you practice gratitude?*

# With Ease

It took me a long time to recognize, understand, and appreciate the value of ease. There are some friends and neighbors I clicked with from the very start. Our connection was seamless. Not to say relationships are easy and don't require effort, they do. But over time I've come to realize that the ones that are effortless and come with ease are meant for me.

When I moved back across the country, it took a while to find a place to settle in but once I did, everything fell into place. I found the ideal residence and signed my lease all in the same week of receiving a job offer. I was grateful and excited for what was next.

*What are some things in your life that happened with ease? How did you feel?*

# When It's Not Working

Then there are things that aren't with ease. Think about a relationship, friendship, or perhaps a job that no matter what you do and how hard you try, it simply does not work.

*Are you in it now or have you moved on? If you've moved on, what are some of your reflections?*

# Supposed-to-be

What I had in mind and in my heart on what my life was "supposed to be" is very different from what actually is. I thought I'd be married to a wonderful partner and a loving mom to two or three kids by now. I have been blessed in other ways though. I've had the opportunity to advance in my career, spend quality time with family and friends, travel to different parts of the world, live in a different part of the country, and adopt new hobbies. I remain hopeful that what was "supposed to be" will happen as it should in due time. But I continue to enjoy my life as it is in the meantime.

*What was your "supposed to be" and has it happened? If not, has not having things work out in the way you imagined caused you to change your vision in any way?*

# I am Open to Receiving

I am naturally a giving person—with my time, thoughts, and resources. I am not used to receiving and honestly, receiving has been uncomfortable until lately. At times I feel lost, confused, and anxious about where I am and where I'm going but other times, the universe and people in my life show up and come through for me when I least expected it. I have friends who text or call consistently just to check in. A good friend that is practically family sent me a book I might enjoy because I was going through something. A neighbor's kid knocked on my door to invite me to dinner with their family one evening. I felt thought of and it brought me joy. It's not easy for me to open up, but I recently shared an experience about my last job not working out to a select few. It wasn't about what happened, but *how* it happened. The people I opened up to were so supportive and I was blown away by how much love and support I felt from them checking on me, sending encouragement, hyping me up over text messages, opening up about their experiences, and the advice.

### *How open are you to receiving?*

# Do it Scared

Someone once told me if you're not failing, then maybe you aren't trying. Doing things you've never done before can be scary. Most of the time, I'm glad I tried regardless of the outcome. From leaving my hometown to move across the country for an adventure, learning how to snowboard as an adult, to taking a solo trip—I'm so glad I did it! I encourage you to do it scared instead of wondering *what if.*

### *What would you like to do scared?*

# Guarded

I've always been a guarded person. I believe being betrayed by an immediate family member that tore my family apart plays a role in my tendency to be guarded, especially with new people and situations that enter my life. Dishonesty, whether big or small, hurts and has had a significant impact on how I navigate the world.

*Are you a guarded person? Why or why not? Has there ever been a situation that caused you to be guarded?*

# Self Check-in

*What are you effortlessly good at doing? What brings you joy?*

# Season of Change

One of my good friends and I usually check in with one another during a change of season, typically Fall and Spring. We've been friends for over twenty years now and we always talk about our seasons of change, what's going on in our lives, and what we are hoping for. Right now, I have a bit of a blank canvas. The job I had didn't work out and now I am figuring out what is next. While it feels like everything is falling apart, perhaps it's falling into place.

I'd like the opportunity to have more control over my time. Work on projects that excite and bring me joy. Prioritize my self-care and mental health. Prioritize my personal life instead of pouring so much of my time and energy into a job. More time to think and be creative. I don't have a plan, which is scary and usually not like me, but maybe I am fundamentally changing too—learning how to be freer and go with the flow.

*Have you or are you currently experiencing a season of change? What did you learn and what are you hoping for in this next chapter?*

# Vulnerability

Admittedly, I'm not good at being vulnerable but I am a work in progress. I don't allow too many people to get to know me, but for some with whom I cross paths, it comes more easily. I guess it has to do with the connection and vibe.

Given my upbringing and life experiences, I'm not sure I've had many opportunities to be vulnerable…or is that just in my head?

My dad's betrayal of my mom tore our family apart and, in the aftermath, I believed I needed to protect my mom emotionally. But who protects me?

***What is your relationship with vulnerability?***

# Going First

"Going first" can be added to the list of things I am working on. When it comes to being open, letting people in, or initiating, I am more comfortable when the other person goes first. I'm grateful to one of my bffs for going first. We've been close for a little more than two years, but it feels like we've been in each other's lives far longer. A lot has happened for both of us since we've known each other and through it all, we've unwaveringly been there for each other, and it brought us closer.

I will never forget the day we met. It was an introduction meeting over a video call. She introduced herself, mentioned that she's a single mom, where she lives and is originally from, and she pointed out our similar work backgrounds. We quickly discovered we have very similar cultural backgrounds and upbringing too. I was shocked that she was this open to someone she just met. I thought, *wow, here is a person that knows herself, owns it, and is never afraid to share.* Her ability to stand in her power and knowledge of self has made me feel safe, comfortable, and willing to reciprocate the openness.

***Do you struggle with going first, or can you do this for someone else?***

# Overthinking

Have you heard of the Enneagram? It's a personality test and I am type 5 —The Investigator.

*a cerebral thinker; seeks knowledge and understanding; loves to learn*

I don't do well with the unknown or what's next, which brings anxiety. When I got mistreated by someone, I spent a lot of time trying to understand why and why it was handled a certain way. I've learned to accept that I may never know the answer.

Overthinking may have led to self-sabotage in certain situations. Nonetheless, I am aware of it and am practicing better habits to manage my overthinking, such as letting things be. A personal mantra: Stop thinking and start feeling. You don't need to intellectualize everything.

**Are there moments where you overthink?**

# Walking Away

It has taken me a while to recognize that a theme from life lessons I've learned is not walking away sooner, especially when I know I deserved better. I come from an immigrant family and a theme I saw and experienced growing up was struggle. My parents working multiple jobs and overtime was the norm. My mom was the alpha parent and main homemaker despite also having a full-time job. I was always encouraged to work really hard. It seemed like hard work and struggle were correlated.

I've struggled through and tolerated certain relationships and work environments longer than I should have. In hindsight, I knew I should have walked away sooner. You deserve better and your gut always knows.

*Have you been in a situation where you saw red flags and stayed? Was your energy or intuition trying to tell you something and you ignored it or put it aside? If so, what finally made things shift?*

# Choose Your Hard

Starting a business is hard. Working in Corporate America is hard. Being unemployed is hard. Being married is hard. Being divorced is hard. Being single is hard.

Life is full of *hard*.

**Which hard do you choose?**

# Healing

Everyone's healing journey is different and usually involves various mini journeys over the course of your life. I've healed in different ways in the past—moving across the country for an adventure, journaling every week, spending time alone, spending time with family and friends, cooking soulfully, walking in nature, laughing, walking on the beach,  going to therapy, the list goes on...

*What are the ways you find healing?*

# Move

There is power in movement. It's good for the body and soul.

I walk in the mornings, hike on weekends, love going to Pilates reformer, play tennis, and go to my boxing gym. Sometimes getting started is a struggle, but I always feel better after I move my body. The strength resonates both physically and mentally.

*How do you step into your power in movement?*

# Finding Peace

A few years ago, a friend and I were journaling on a beach during the first week of January. She asked me what was my one word theme for the year. PEACE was the first thing that came to mind. I understand the importance of finding and protecting my peace now more than ever before. I notice when I'm at peace, I'm at ease mentally, physically, and emotionally.

*When are you at peace? How will you intentionally try to make decisions for your life that bring you peace?*

# Soft Era

I am exhausted from the grind, and hustle culture. Trying to do a million things, working on multiple goals at once, and maintaining an intense to-do nature is too much.

I want to embrace a softer era in this next chapter where things are calmer, more peaceful, at ease, and I have time to think and enjoy the moment. I've been go-go-go in non-stop chaotic environments and that's not how I want to operate or how I want to be. I want to be gentler with myself and learn how to relax.

***What would your soft era look like?***

# Why Not

*Why Not* has been a theme over the last year. Being an Enneagram 5 (deep thinker), I would question everything, especially something I've never done before. I used to spend more time coming up with reasons why I shouldn't do something instead of doing it. Snowboarding is an injury-prone hobby, hard to learn, pricey, and it involves being outdoors in the freezing cold, but something I've always wanted to do. So, I started snowboarding this year. I've gone from falling frequently to falling half of the time. The point is, I'm glad I started.

I am also exploring working for myself. It's a different type of hustle. My friend encouraged me to explore this by reaching out to people, even ones I don't know, to get their perspective and learn about their journey. He said, get used to no response and rejection, but all it takes is one. Again, why not? I've reached out to twenty people so far, three responded and two turned into networking conversations. You just never know where these conversations could lead. And it wasn't as scary and impossible as I originally thought. I encourage you to try or get started, because *why not.*

***What's something you've always wanted to do? What's holding you back?***

# Micro Changes

One of my mentors once told me that nothing changes if nothing changes. If I didn't like what was going on in my life, identify the things that I can control and start making micro changes so things start to shift. From starting to take walks in the morning, trying a new workout class that could turn into a regular habit, going to bed earlier, reading a book instead of watching tv, I'm constantly trying to make micro changes.

Identify the little shifts you can make throughout your day that will give you a different perspective and energy, and things will start to change.

***What are some micro changes you can do?***

# Outgrown

Growth also means outgrowing current situations, people, and places. When you are evolving and elevating, there are people, situations, and places that no longer serve you. Maybe you are holding onto something or letting something take up space that isn't pouring into you anymore.

*If you're being really honest with yourself, what have you outgrown?*

# In Your Favor

I believe now more than ever that everything is happening in my favor—*for* me and not to me.

It's time for us to be aware and start living life like everything is working out in our favor. I think about the opportunities I didn't get, friendships and relationships that have ended, and situations that ended quickly. Rejection is redirection.  It was all working in my favor. This works both ways too. I am grateful for the people that have come into my life, projects that happened, and trips I took. They were all in my favor and right on time.

*Tell me something that ended up working in your favor.*

# Decide

Don't underestimate the power of intention. Making decisions is both deciding what to do and not do. I will not tolerate disrespect. I will walk away when I know I deserve better to protect my peace.

*What are some things you are deciding on?*

# Moments of Joy

A good friend and I often talk about stringing little moments of joy. Even when things seem heavy or we aren't where we want to be, we can still find moments that bring us joy.

Simply spending time with my sister even when we aren't doing much brings me so much joy. Saying yes to social invites and attending little league baseball, softball, and youth soccer games bring me joy. Simply connecting with genuinely kindhearted people brings me joy. Doing little things to help others brings me joy.

*What are some moments that bring you joy? How can you spread your joy to others?*

# Surrender

Surrendering is a big one. However, acknowledging it and doing it are different things. I've gotten better at surrendering and am more comfortable doing it with flow and ease. Things haven't gone as planned and are still unknown. Not knowing is tough for an overthinker, but I'm learning how to enjoy it and not stress like I usually would.

Let it be and let things unfold. Be in flow.

*What comes to mind when you think of surrendering? In what areas of your life have you found yourself less willing to surrender?*

# Blessings

I am blessed.

While things aren't perfect and my life isn't what I had imagined it to be at this point, I know that I am blessed given the people in my life and the opportunities I've had.

***In what ways are you blessed?***

# Grounding

Are there certain people, routines, or places that help keep you grounded? For me, it's being around genuinely kind people, traveling to get out of my usual environment from time to time, listening to music, journaling, and going for walks. It doesn't take much, but I must commit to these things so I don't lose the habit. I need to make time.

***What keeps you grounded?***

# Let Go and Trust

I am getting better at letting go and trusting. Typically, I'm a go-getter and operate by doing. There is less anxiety when I have some control. I didn't really know how to sit back and let things unfold and simply trust that a higher plan is unfolding. I came to realize that when I stopped seeing letting go and trusting as scary, I was calmer and more at peace. It's like a switch went off one day.

*What are some things you'd like to just let go and trust?*

# Soulmates

Do you know you can have more than one soulmate? While it can be a romantic partner, it could also be a friend or family member. A soulmate is about a deep soul connection. I haven't always known this distinction but once I learned about it, I realized that I've been blessed with quite a few, especially soul sisters.

***Who are your soulmates?***

# Don't Put Things Off. Just Start.

Isn't it funny that you can follow through and do everything for other people or your job, but when it comes to the bucket list things you want to do for yourself, you often procrastinate and find reasons to put it off? So, Coldplay is my favorite band. My roommate from when I lived in NYC, who is like a sister to me, and I always wanted to see Coldplay internationally. Well, I just started a new job and was hesitant to take time off to travel to Europe for a show. She reminded me that this is on the bucket list and we need to live and do things we want to do and say we will do. We ended up going to Europe to see Coldplay! Even better, she invited two other friends and we had the best time. This was during a time when I really needed to start healing and reset because of a not-so-great experience. I was going to be thousands of miles away from home, wanted to be present, and leave everything behind temporarily. I'm so glad I didn't pass on the trip. I'll never forget it.

*What's on your bucket list and when will you tackle the next thing? What's stopping you?*

# You Never Know

I don't see myself as an author and never thought I'd actually publish a journal. I write in my journal weekly and this has helped me get grounded and express what I'm thinking and feeling. It all started with deciding to try because *why not* and *you never know.* Leaning in with that attitude is why you're holding this book in your hands. It all worked out. I sometimes wonder, what if I didn't try? But I'm so glad I did. I encourage you to do one thing you've always wanted or simply start because...*you never know.*

**What is one thing you've always wanted to do?**

# Anything Can Happen
# (At Any Time)

Sometimes "it" just finds you so expect the unexpected.

*Has something just happened for you out of nowhere like meeting and connecting with a soul mate out of the blue, getting sought after for a job opportunity that hasn't been posted yet, or something else?*

# Just Say Yes

One of my best friends and I often talk about being in our "just say yes" era. From an invite for a social gathering to taking a trip, or something else, we are committed to the idea of just going with a yes instead of thinking of all the reasons to say no. So often, great things happen because of a yes.

*When was a time you said yes and how has that shaped your ability to find the value in choosing yes?*

# When You're Ready

It's okay to not do everything at once. I often struggle with the perception of timelines and where I think I should be at a given point in time. Sometimes I reflect on my intention in a given situation and realized that my actions didn't reflect the outcome I wanted. For example, I wanted to have more balance with time for my personal life, but I kept taking jobs that were high stress and demanding which made setting work boundaries difficult. You'll notice things start coming into your life when you're ready for it.

*What are you ready for now? And if you are being honest with yourself, how do you know you're actually ready?*

# In Flow

I'm a planner by nature. I want to be more spontaneous and go with the flow. In retrospect, a lot of the best things that have happened in my life are when I'm in flow.

Some things you can control. Others you cannot.

I'm so grateful I've leaned into opportunities that have come into my life even though some weren't exactly what I wanted at the time.

***How does it feel when you're in the flow?***

# Procrastination

Procrastinating doesn't mean you're lazy. It could be associated with fear, unpleasant feelings, negative emotions, or avoiding tasks that make you feel frustrated. If you sometimes procrastinate, try to avoid judging yourself.

This is small and silly. I'm a huge procrastinator when it comes to packing for a trip. I love traveling, don't get me wrong, but thinking about what to pack and trying to make it all fit in my suitcase gives me anxiety. Am I over packing? Probably. Am I forgetting something? Maybe.

***Can you relate? Big or small—what are you procrastinating about and why?***

# Time Off

Take that vacation. Take a mental health day. Take a walk. Take a gap in between jobs.

I didn't realize how burnt out I was from working 12 to 15-hour days and bothered by work on the weekends. But the truth is, I allowed it.

***Real talk: Do you need to take a break? If so, what would you do if you had the time off?***

# When Nothing is Certain, Everything is Possible

While things have not turned out how I imagined, maybe it's not such a bad thing. I can have a new chapter that is more in the flow and customized for me. I can do whatever I want, even if that means doing it scared. I just need to reset and refocus. While it's incredibly scary, it's exciting. I have no plans, leaving more time to discover myself and make some.

*If you had the opportunity to (re)write a new chapter, what would it be?*

# Openness

I usually have a strong opinion. Because of life just life-ing and things happening that are out of my control, it's a forcing mechanism to stay open. Luckily, I have a great support system that encourages me every day *to stay open.*

**If you were truly open, what would you invite to come into your life?**

# Invest in Yourself

We often spend time, energy, and money investing in people and random things but do you invest in yourself? Get your yoga teacher certification, open that business, take time off to heal, go back to school, find time to work out or take that trip. Whatever it is that you want to do, don't forget about *you*.

**How will you start investing in yourself?**

# Support System

Despite life's challenges, I have always been blessed and am forever grateful for my support system. I'm naturally guarded, but there are people who accept me for who I am and make me feel safe enough to open up and be vulnerable. There are people who I speak to daily and others where we pick up where we left off. I'm fortunate enough to have people in my life who are always there, regardless of the timing and situation. No matter what's going on, even if we don't talk every day, whenever I need them, they are always there (even if not in proximity).

*Who are these people for you? What role/significance does your support system play in your life? If you don't have a support system, what first step can you take in creating one?*

# Let Them

Let people be who they are so they can show you who they really are. Don't expect people to change. In turn, you should always be your authentic self. Here's the thing, if you are trying to change someone for the idea of who you want them to be, that dynamic might lead to disappointment in the long run. Take your time and get to know someone authentically. In addition to chemistry, compatibility and connection, don't forget about character. Try to step back and see how things unfold.

*Would letting them be hard for you?*

# Energy Check

I was in multiple jobs that I dreaded. The work I did and people I worked with were great for the most part (nothing is perfect), but the issue was in how we operated. Eventually, this caught up to me and I burnt out. I probably wasn't showing up as my best self anymore either. It's also not healthy to be in situations that are draining and exhausting.

*So, energy check. Whether it's a situation or relationship, how would you describe how being in it makes you feel?*

# From Now On

We often make promises to ourselves. Those promises should build us up and help us be the best version of ourselves.

I promised myself that from now on, I will make choices that align with the vision of my authentic self. I will prioritize my self-care and mental health. I will slow down and do things intentionally that align with who I want to be, how I want to operate, and how I want to live my life. I will invest in things that are good for my soul.

Now it's your turn.

***From now on I will:***

*Thank you for letting me share part of my journey and allowing me to be part of yours. Keep going, glowing, and growing.*

www.ingramcontent.com/pod-product-compliance
Lightning Source LLC
Chambersburg PA
CBHW051639120626
46551CB00014B/2145